SHEET MUSIC FOR CLASSICAL PIANO: BACH, MOZART, BEETHOVEN AND THEIR MASTERPIECES

A JOURNEY THROUGH THE WORKS OF THE THREE GIANT AND MOST CELEBRATED CLASSICAL MUSIC COMPOSERS IN HISTORY

VOLUME 2

ISBN: 978-1-80221-020-0

Content

- Sonata for Piano No. 14 in C-sharp minor, Op. 27, No. 2 by Beethoven ….Page 4
- Sonata for Piano No. 16 in C Major, K. 545 ("Sonata facile") by Mozart.Page 19
- Prelude and Fugue in B-flat Major, BWV 866 by Bach ……………..Page 30
- Prelude and Fugue in B Minor, BWV 869 by Bach……...…………Page 35
- Prelude and Fugue in B-flat Minor, BWV 867 by Bach………….…Page 44
- Sonata for Piano No. 24 in F-sharp Major, Op. 78 by Beethoven………..Page 49
- Prelude and Fugue in A Major, BWV 864 by Bach……………….....Page 60
- Sonata for Piano No. 3 in B-flat Major, K. 281/189f by Mozart………… Page 65
- Prelude and Fugue in E Major, BWV 854 by Bach………………….Page 84
- Sonata for Piano No. 12 in A-flat Major, Op. 26 by Beethoven………….Page 88
- Prelude and Fugue in A Minor, BWV 865 by Bach……………....…Page 106
- Prelude and Fugue in C Major, BWV 846 by Bach………………....…Page 116

Piano Sonata No. 14 in C-sharp minor, Op. 27, No. 2
("Moonlight Sonata")
by
Ludwig van Beethoven.

This is one of Beethoven's most famous and beloved works, with its "Adagio sostenuto" movement becoming particularly iconic

SONATE.

Op. 27. № 2.

(Sonata quasi una Fantasia.)

Der Gräfin Julie Guicciardi gewidmet.

Adagio sostenuto.

Si deve suonare tutto questo pezzo delicatissimamente e senza sordini.

14.

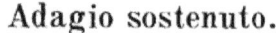

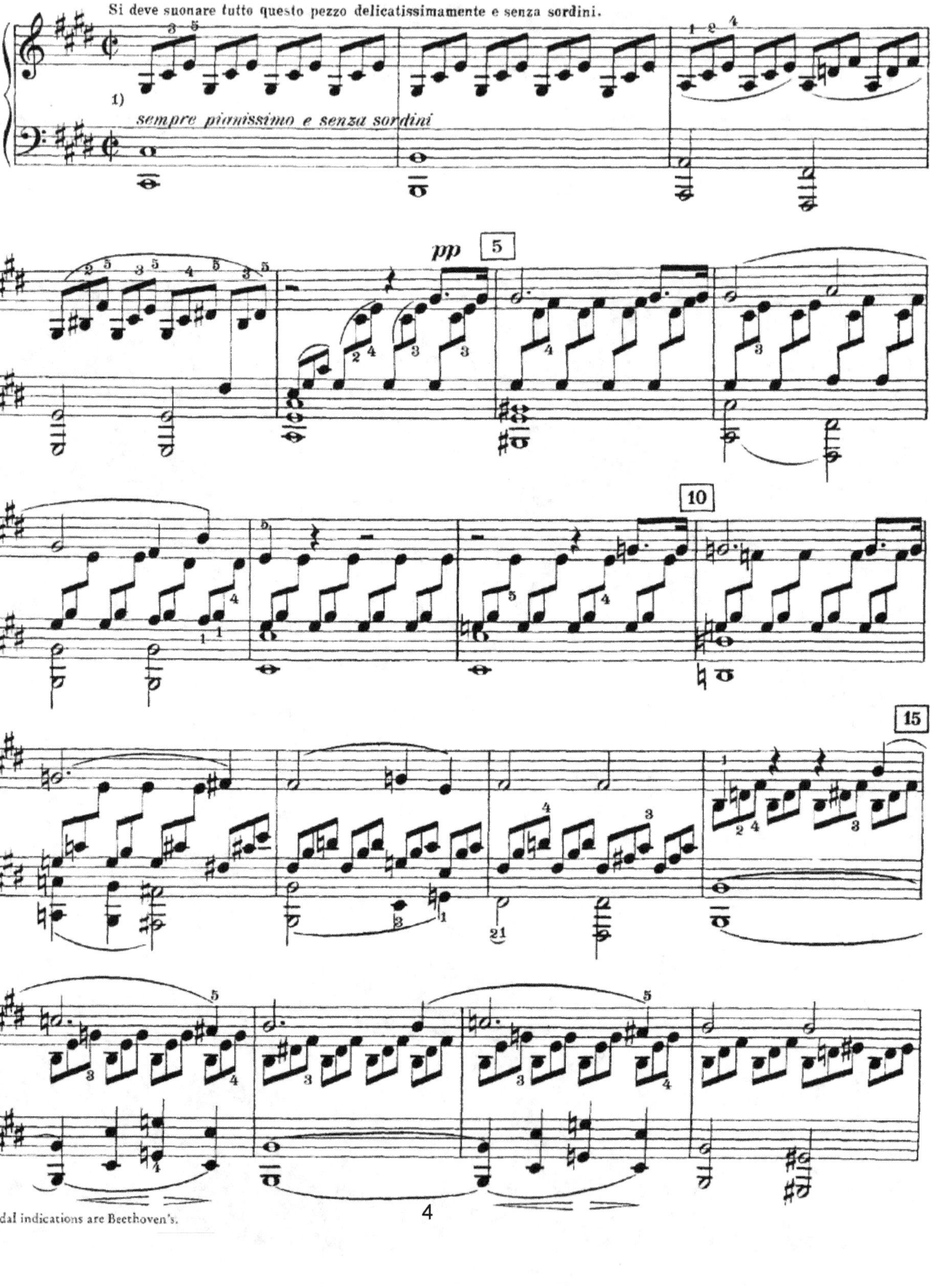

1) The pedal indications are Beethoven's.

Presto agitato.

Piano Sonata No. 16 in C Major, K. 545
by
Wolfgang Amadeus Mozart.
Also known as the "Sonata facile," it is one of Mozart's most performed and studied works for piano.

SONATA FACILE

Köchel Nr. 545

Prelude and Fugue in B-flat Major, BWV 866
(from "Book I of The Well-Tempered Clavier")
Concludes Bach's series of preludes and fugues with another significant example of his compositional genius.

Preludio XXI.

Fuga XXI.
a 3 Voci.

Allegro vivace. ($\bullet$ = 116.)

Prelude and Fugue in B Minor, BWV 869
(from "Book I of The Well-Tempered Clavier")
Another impressive example of Bach's counterpoint, offering challenges and interpretive beauty.

Preludio XXIV.

Fuga XXIV.
a 4 Voci.

Prelude and Fugue in B-flat Minor, BWV 867
(from "Book I of The Well-Tempered Clavier")
Another example of contrapuntal mastery, with the prelude and fugue unfolding intricately and engagingly.

Preludio XXII.

Fuga XXII.
a 5 Voci.

Piano Sonata No. 24 in F-sharp Major, Op. 78
by
Ludwig van Beethoven.

Also known as the "Piano Sonata in F-sharp Major," this short but intense work is admired for its delicacy and sense of emotional expression.

SONATE.

Op. 78.

Der Gräfin Therese von Brunswick gewidmet.

Componiert im Oktober 1809.

24. Adagio cantabile.   Allegro ma non troppo.

---

1) The fingering in italics and the pedal indications are Beethoven's.
2) Here, in contrast to Op. 54 (cf. 1st movement, mm. 18, 20 & 24), a true *prallender Doppelschlag* is wanted:
3) In the autograph and original edition (Breitkopf & Härtel) the l. h. has g instead of f𝄪 in this measure and the next.

1) See footnote to m. 17. 2) In the autograph and original edition the l. h. has c instead of b♯.

1) It is unacceptable here to repeat the f♯ of the second quarter-beat, since the third g¹–c² has motivic significance; see the thirds e²–c♯², d²–b¹ and b¹–g♯² in the following measures.

1) The l. h. over the r. h.

1) This measure, in a way, amounts to four 8ths: C♯, c♮, c♯¹ and the 8th-rest.

Prelude and Fugue in A Major, BWV 864
(from "Book I of The Well-Tempered Clavier")
Continues Bach's series of preludes and fugues, offering another opportunity to explore the musical richness of his compositions.

Preludio XIX.

Fuga XIX.
a 3 Voci.

Piano Sonata No. 3 in B-flat Major, K. 281/189f

by

Wolfgang Amadeus Mozart.

This sonata showcases Mozart's melodic vein and typical formal elegance in his music.

SONATE

Allegro moderato

W. A. Mozart
Köchel Nr. 281

Rondeau
Allegro

41

42

Prelude and Fugue in E Major, BWV 854

(from "Book I of The Well-Tempered Clavier"). Another gem from Bach's repertoire, showcasing his ability to create beauty and complexity through the forms of prelude and fugue.

Preludio IX.

Fuga IX.
a 3 Voci.

Allegro vivace. (♩=108.)

Piano Sonata No. 12 in A-flat Major, Op. 26
by
Ludwig van Beethoven.

Also known as the "Piano Sonata in A-flat Major," this work is celebrated for its variety of movements and emotional depth.

SONATE.
Op. 81ª
Das Lebewohl.

Bei der Abreise S.K. Hoheit des verehrten Erzherzogs Rudolph. Wien, am 21. Mai 1809.

*) "On the departure of H. M. the revered Archduke Rudolph. Vienna, May 21, 1809." (The French entered Vienna in 1809.) In opposition to Beethoven's specific instructions, the original edition bears a title he complained of several times: "Sonate caractéristique: Les adieux, l'absence, et le retour" (The Farewell, The Absence, The Return—Das Lebewohl, Abwesenheit, Wiedersehen).

1) The fingering in italics and the pedal indications are Beethoven's.

1) In the autograph there is a *p* here too, in place of the erased >

1) The slur here follows the autograph and the original edition in its difference from mm 23 & 24

1) Here the slur is once more like mm 23 & 24, again on the basis of the autograph original edition.

1) d^2 in the l. h. chord according to the autograph.

Abwesenheit.
Andante espressivo.
In gehender Bewegung, doch mit Ausdruck.

1) Execute the ornament (*prallender Doppelschlag*) before the second 8th-beat
2) Execute the ornament on the fourth 32nd-beat
3) Beethoven was obviously thinking of a *prallender Doppelschlag* ornamented in trill-like fashion

Wiedersehen.
Vivacissimamente.
Im lebhaftesten Zeitmaasse.

Im Januar 1810.

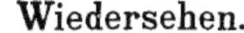

1) Trill with the Nachschlag $bb^1 c^2$.

Prelude and Fugue in A Minor, BWV 865

(from "Book I of The Well-Tempered Clavier").

Another demonstration of Bach's compositional mastery, with the prelude and fugue intertwining intricately and engagingly.

Preludio XX.

Fuga XX.

a 4 Voci.

Fuga XX.

a 4 Voci.

Prelude and Fugue in C Major, BWV 846
(from "Book I of The Well-Tempered Clavier").
This piece is among the most famous and frequently played compositions
by
Johann Sebastian Bach.

Part First.
Preludio I.

All figures in the fingering which are set above the notes are intended, whether in inner or outer parts, for the right hand; whereas, the figures below the notes are for the left hand. This explanation will suffice to show, in doubtful cases, by which hand any note in the inner parts is to be played.

Alle Fingersatz-Zahlen, welche über den Noten stehen, gelten (auch in den Mittelstimmen) stets der rechten Hand. Dagegen sind die unter den Noten stehenden Zahlen immer für die linke Hand bestimmt. Dieses reicht hin, um in zweifelhaften Fällen anzuzeigen, von welcher Hand jede Note in den Mittelstimmen gegriffen werden muss.

Fuga I.
a 4 Voci.

www.ingramcontent.com/pod-product-compliance
Lightning Source LLC
Chambersburg PA
CBHW082210070526
44585CB00020B/2358